YAKUZA VS. MAFIA

Disclaimer:

The battles in this book are not real. It is fun to imagine. These 2 opponents would never fight each other in real life.

45th Parallel Press

Published in the United States of America by Cherry Lake Publishing
Ann Arbor, Michigan
www.cherrylakepublishing.com

Reading Adviser: Marla Conn, MS, Ed., Literacy specialist, Read-Ability, Inc.
Book Designer: Melinda Millward

Photo Credits: © TCD/Prod.DB/Alamy Stock Photo, cover, 5; © Lorado/istock, back cover, cover, 5, 10, 15, 16; © Aseph/Shutterstock.com, 6; © track5/istock, 9; © Dmitrijs Mihejevs/Shutterstock.com, 12; © GraphicsRF/Shutterstock.com, 19, 20; © AtomStudios/istock, 19; © vectortatu/Shutterstock.com, 20; © SasaStock/Shutterstock.com, 21; © Pelevina Ksinia/Shutterstock.com, 23; © Nikola Knezevic/Shutterstock.com, 24; © gyro/istock, 25; © Dalaifood/Shutterstock.com, 25; © Nastasic/istock, 27; © Everett Collection/age fotostock, 29

Graphic Element Credits: © studiostoks/Shutterstock.com, back cover, multiple interior pages; © infostocker/Shutterstock.com, back cover, multiple interior pages; © mxbfilms/Shutterstock.com, front cover; © MF production/Shutterstock.com, front cover, multiple interior pages; © AldanNi/Shutterstock.com, front cover, multiple interior pages; © Andrii Symonenko/Shutterstock.com, front cover, multiple interior pages; © acidmit/Shutterstock.com, front cover, multiple interior pages; © manop/Shutterstock.com, multiple interior pages; © Lina Kalina/Shutterstock.com, multiple interior pages; © mejorana/Shutterstock.com, multiple interior pages; © NoraVector/Shutterstock.com, multiple interior pages; © Smirnov Viacheslav/Shutterstock.com, multiple interior pages; © Piotr Urakau/Shutterstock.com, multiple interior pages; © IMOGI graphics/Shutterstock.com, multiple interior pages; © jirawat phueksriphan/Shutterstock.com, multiple interior pages

45th Parallel Press is an imprint of Cherry Lake Publishing.

Library of Congress Cataloging-in-Publication Data

Names: Loh-Hagan, Virginia, author.
Title: Yakuza vs. Mafia / by Virginia Loh-Hagan.
Other titles: Yakuza versus mafia
Description: Ann Arbor : Cherry Lake Publishing, [2019] | Series: Battle royale: lethal warriors | Includes bibliographical references and index.
Identifiers: LCCN 2019003646| ISBN 9781534147690 (hardcover) | ISBN 9781534149120 (pdf) | ISBN 9781534150553 (pbk.) | ISBN 9781534151987 (hosted ebook)
Subjects: LCSH: Organized crime–Juvenile literature. | Mafia–Juvenile literature. | Yakuza–Juvenile literature.
Classification: LCC HV6441 .L64 2019 | DDC 364.106–dc23
LC record available at https://lccn.loc.gov/2019003646

Printed in the United States of America
Corporate Graphics

About the Author

Dr. Virginia Loh-Hagan is an author, university professor, former classroom teacher, and curriculum designer. She loves Chicago. She discovered Italian beef sandwiches there. She lives in San Diego with her very tall husband and very naughty dogs. To learn more about her, visit www.virginialoh.com.

Table of Contents

Introduction

Imagine a battle between Yakuza and the American **mafia**. Mafia means mob. Who would win? Who would lose?

Enter the world of *Battle Royale: Lethal* **Warriors**! Warriors are fighters. This is a fight to the death! The last team standing is the **victor**! Victors are winners. They get to live.

Opponents are fighters who compete against each other. They challenge each other. They fight with everything they've got. They use weapons. They use their special skills. They use their powers.

They're not fighting for prizes. They're not fighting for honor. They're not fighting for their countries. They're fighting for their lives. Victory is their only option.

Let the games begin!

In real life, nobody really wins in a war.

YAKUZA

Many Yakuza members are of Korean descent. Descent has to do with where a family is from.

Yakuza is the Japanese mafia. It's organized crime gangs. The members are called gangsters or mobsters. They do **illegal** things. Illegal means against the law. Yakuza gamble. They sell people. They sell drugs and guns. They **smuggle**. Smuggle means to bring things in and out of countries. Yakuza **bribe**. Bribe means to pay people money to do things for them. They **blackmail**. Blackmail means to demand money for not telling secrets. Yakuza loan people money. They charge them a lot of fees.

They make a lot of money. They're sneaky. They create real businesses. They use these businesses to **launder** money. Launder is to hide money made from illegal work. This keeps lawmen away.

Yakuza have been around for a long time. It started in the early 17th century when tekiya and bakuto appeared. They were traveling salesmen. They traveled around Japan. They were gamblers. They tricked buyers. They formed into groups. This paved the way for the Yakuza.

Some Yakuza think they came from ronin. Ronin were samurai warriors who didn't serve masters. Some Yakuza may have come from the kabukimono. Kabukimono were the "crazy ones." They were street gangs. They dressed in bright colors. They robbed people. They didn't pay their bills. They got into fights.

There are many different gangs. Gangs have different names. They have different leaders. The top boss is called kumicho.

Some Yakuza are outcasts and orphans. They're people who have no families.

Yakuza are loyal to their gangs. They have a code of conduct. They believe in honor. They obey their bosses. In return, they get protection. If Yakuza disobey, they're punished. They can be killed. They can be kicked out.

A popular punishment is yubitsume. The boss gives the mobster a knife and bandage. The mobster chops off his pinky finger. He gives it to the boss. This weakens the mobster's ability to hold weapons. More fingers can be cut off if needed.

Yakuza punish people who don't pay them back. They punish people who don't do what they want. They shoot them. They beat them up.

FUN FACTS ABOUT YAKUZA

- Yakuza are named after a Japanese card game. Players draw 3 cards. Cards must add up to 9. The worst cards are 8, 9, and 3. Ya is 8. Ku is 9. Sa is 3.
- In 1995, there was an earthquake in Japan. In 2011, there was a tsunami in Japan. Tsunamis are sea wave storms. Yakuza were among the first to help with both. They sent boats. They sent helicopters. They sent supplies.
- A Yakuza group created a newsletter. The newsletter was sent to over 28,000 members. It including fishing tips. It included haiku. Haiku are Japanese poems. Yakuza numbers have been decreasing. They thought the newsletter was a way to get more support. They wanted to separate themselves from violence.
- In 2009, a Yakuza group wanted its members to know about laws. An exam was created. It was 12 pages.
- The first Yakuza members may have been like Robin Hood. Hood stole from the rich. He gave money to the poor. Yakuza defended their towns. They fought against robbers.

MAFIA

Mafia groups are also in New York City and Las Vegas.

The American mafia is very similar to Yakuza. They're criminals. They commit the same crimes. They do illegal things. They run from the law.

There are many mafia groups in the United States. They're mainly in big cities. The most famous mafia group is the Chicago **Outfit**. Outfit means group or team. The Chicago Outfit mobsters are Italian Americans. They are the biggest and most powerful.

Mafia groups fight in bloody gang wars. Gangs fight for **territory**. Territories are areas. Gangs fight for power. They want control. They hurt people. They rob. They destroy homes and stores. They **extort**. Extort means to get money by force. People have to pay the mafia to leave them alone.

Mobsters will do anything to carry out their crimes. They'll do anything to protect their gangs. They see each other as family members. The top boss is called the godfather.

Mobsters have a code of silence. They don't tell on each other. They take betrayal seriously. For example, a mobster was tricked by an undercover cop. He introduced the cop to mafia members. The truth came out. The mobster was killed. His hands were cut off. This is because he let the cop shake hands with mafia bosses.

Mobsters are violent. They mainly use guns. But they'll use any weapons. An example is **brass knuckles**. Brass knuckles are metal rings worn over knuckles. They make punches hurt more.

Another term for the mafia is "cosa nostra." This is Italian for "our way." It's about being a family.

Mobsters **threaten**. Threaten means to warn people by scaring them. Mobsters tell people they're going to hurt them. For example, a popular method was started by an Italian gang called the Black Hand. They can be traced back to Naples in the 1750s. Mafia members would sign a letter with a black hand print. This meant people needed to pay up or get hurt.

Mobsters **torture**. Torture means to cause pain on purpose. Mobsters perform **hits**. Hits are killing jobs. Godfathers give orders for hits.

Mobsters do a lot of their business in restaurants. They own restaurants. They meet in restaurants. They kill enemies in restaurants. Some restaurants have underground tunnels. This is for easy escape.

FUN FACTS ABOUT THE AMERICAN MAFIA

- Joseph Colombo was a mafia boss. He lived in Brooklyn, New York. He started the Italian-American Civil Rights League. He felt the FBI was mistreating him. He didn't like how Italians were being depicted in the movies.

- In 2011, the FBI took down over 120 mobsters. This was the "largest mob roundup in FBI history." Over 800 federal, state, and local officials worked on this.

- Some mobsters had funny names. There was Vinny Carwash. There was Johnny Pizza. There was Jack the Whack.

- "Turncoat mobsters" help the FBI. They wear wires. They give information. They make deals. They help put mobsters in jail.

- In the 1940s and 1950s, the Los Angeles Police Department created the Gangster Squad. Eight cops worked on this. They fought against the mafia. They spied on bad cops.

- Ella Fitzgerald was a famous singer. At age 15, she worked for the mafia. She worked as a player in an illegal lottery game. She was caught. She was sent to a reform school.

CHOOSE YOUR BATTLEGROUND

Yakuza and the American mafia are very similar. They have the same goals. They're organized in the same way. They harm and kill on order. They don't think twice about hurting others. Their loyalty is to their mob families. Yakuza and the mafia are well-matched. They're equal in skills. Choose your battleground carefully!

Battleground #1: Sea

- Yakuza live in Japan. Japan is an **island**. Islands are surrounded by water. Yakuza should know how to live off the sea.

- The American mafia live in the United States. They mainly live in big **urban** areas. Urban means city life. Most big cities are close to **ports**. Ports are where ships come in and out.

The mafia can trace their history to Sicilian mobs. Sicily is an island in Italy.

Battleground #2: Land

• Fighting on land would be easy. Yakuza are well-connected. They have eyes and ears everywhere. Japan is a small country. This makes it easier to know things.

• The mafia are also well-connected. They have large networks. Mob families are also tied to each other. They make **pacts**. Pacts are contracts.

Battleground #3: Mountains

• Over 70 percent of Japan has mountains. Its mountains have a lot of forests. This means that Yakuza are used to fighting on **rugged** lands. Rugged means rocky and uneven.

• The mafia go to the mountains to hide. There aren't many mafia families in mountains. But there are some.

ARMED AND DANGEROUS: WEAPONS

Yakuza: Japan has very strict gun control laws. People get punished for using guns. The punishment is high. Some Yakuza are willing to use fake guns. They only use real guns if they mean to kill. They don't use real guns to make threats. Fake guns still scare people. Yakuza don't want any trouble. They don't want to get caught. The crime isn't worth jail time.

Mafia: Mafia members use Molotov cocktails. Molotov cocktails are homemade bombs. A glass bottle is filled with gas or alcohol. A cloth or sock is stuffed in. It's lit on fire. It's thrown into buildings or cars. It flies in the air. It explodes upon contact. This causes a distraction. It's also a way for the mafia to send a warning. Molotov cocktails are illegal. The United States considers them to be "destructive devices." They're unsafe. They can cause a lot of harm.

FIGHT ON!

The battle begins! Yakuza and the mafia are fighting for power. They are fighting for rights over a new area. They want more money. They need more people to pay **tributes**. Tributes are payments. People pay mobs. Mobs stay away. They don't hurt people who pay.

Move 1:

Mafia members spy. They learn where the Yakuza are staying. They get in a car. They throw a brick at the kumicho's room. The brick breaks his window. A note is wrapped around the brick. The note reads, "Stay away. You've been warned." Mobsters drive away quickly. Their car wheels squeal. They burn rubber.

Many Yakuza join when they're in their teens.

Move 2:

Yakuza want to get even. They pack their machine guns. They get into their car. They follow the mafia. They pretend to **retreat**. Retreat means to give up. They pull out of sight. They follow slowly. They watch the mafia. They see the mafia go into a restaurant. They call the rest of the gang. They tell them where they are.

Move 3:

The mafia gets ready. They know Yakuza will show up soon. They don't know when. They get shotguns. They saw off the tops of shotguns. This makes the shotgun easier to handle. It's used in small spaces. It's dangerous. The bullets scatter. They spread out.

Mafia comes from "mafioso." It means a person who doesn't trust authority.

LIFE SOURCE: FOOD FOR BATTLE

Yakuza: Yakuza eat Japanese food. Shabu shabu is a popular dish. People share food. In the middle, there's a pot of steaming hot broth. There are dishes of vegetables. There are dishes of meat. People use chopsticks. They pick up food. They dip in the hot broth. Food is cooked piece by piece. It's cooked at the table. Shabu shabu means "swish swish." This is the sound of the food in the hot broth.

Mafia: The mafia has Italian roots. So, Italian food is very popular. Al Capone was a famous mobster. His favorite food was spaghetti with walnut sauce. Capone liked extra-long noodles. The sauce was simple. It had oil, walnut pieces, garlic, tomato bits, and Parmesan cheese. Salt and pepper were added. Capone liked tomato sauces too. He called sauces "gravy."

Move 4:

Yakuza **snipers** set up outside the restaurant. Snipers shoot from a hiding place. They have good aim. They can shoot from far away. Yakuza wait for the mafia to come out. The mafia doesn't come out. A Yakuza member goes in.

Move 5:

The mafia recognizes the **tattoos**. Tattoos are ink drawings on skin. Yakuza have tattoos all over their bodies. The mafia shoots their shotguns.

Move 6:

The Yakuza member gets hit. Yakuza want to get the mafia out. They grab smoke bombs. A Yakuza member goes to the door. Snipers cover him. The Yakuza member tosses in the smoke bomb.

Both Yakuza and the mafia come from all classes. Some are poor. Some are rich.

AND THE VICTOR IS . . .

What are their next moves?
Who do you think would win?

Yakuza could win if:

- They cut off the mafia's connections. There are more mafia than Yakuza members. The United States is a lot bigger than Japan. The mafia is connected around the world. Yakuza is mainly in Asia, the United States, and Canada.
- They cut off the mafia's money. The Mafia makes a lot more money. Without it, they can't buy more weapons. They can't bribe more people.

Mafia could win if:

- They break apart the Yakuza **clans**. Clans are families. Since Japan is small, Yakuza gangs are closer. They can work together faster and better.
- They stay away from Japan. Separate the Yakuza from their resources.

Both Yakuza and the mafia make political connections.

Yakuza: Top Champion

Masahisa Takenaka lived from 1933 to 1985. He was the fourth boss of the Yamaguchi-Gumi. Yamaguchi-Gumi is Japan's largest Yakuza gang. It started as a union of dockworkers. The third boss made this Yakuza into one of the world's biggest criminal organizations. He died. His heir died in jail. The Yakuza needed a boss. In 1984, Takenaka was voted in. This made Hiroshi Yamamoto mad. He wanted to be the boss. He broke off. He started his own gang. He took over 3,000 gang members. There was a lot of tension between the two gangs. In 1985, Takenaka went to his girlfriend's house. He was waiting for an elevator. He and three other people were shot dead. This led to a Yakuza war. The war was called the Yama-Ichi War. This war lasted 4 years. Over 36 gangsters died. Many were hurt. There were about 220 gun battles.

Mafia: Top Champion

Al Capone lived from 1899 to 1947. His parents immigrated from Naples, Italy. He was born in New York. At age 14, he hit a teacher. So, he quit school. He worked odd jobs. He worked at a candy story. He worked at a bowling alley. He joined gangs. He got into fights. He killed another gang member. He had to escape. He moved to Chicago. He led the Chicago Outfit from 1925 to 1931. He opened illegal businesses. He made a lot of money. He was part of the St. Valentine's Day Massacre. Massacres are killings of a group of people. Capone's gang dressed up like cops. They lined up gang members. They put them against a wall. They shot at them. Capone was caught in 1931. He didn't pay taxes. He was jailed at Alcatraz. Alcatraz is a prison. It's on an island. It's in San Francisco. Capone got sick. He died in his Florida home.

Consider This!

THINK ABOUT IT!

- How are the Yakuza and the mafia alike? How are they different? Are they more alike or different? Why do you think so?
- Would the Yakuza and the mafia ever fight each other? If so, who do you think would in? Why do you think so?
- What do you think about organized crime? How can we stop it? What has been done in the past?
- Learn more about ninjas. Learn more about samurais. How are they like Yakuza? How are they different? Explain your thinking.
- Have you seen a mafia movie or TV show? What happened? How were the mafia portrayed?

LEARN MORE!

- Johnson, C.M. *Organized Crime*. Fremont, CA: Full Tilt Press, 2017.
- Matthews, Rupert, and Mark Bergin (illust.). *You Wouldn't Want to Be a Chicago Gangster!: Some Dangerous Characters You'd Better Avoid*. New York, NY: Franklin Watts, 2010.
- Mooney, Carla. *Investigating the Mafia*. Detroit, MI: Lucent Books, 2010.
- Roxburgh, Ellis. *Al Capone vs. Eliot Ness: Opposite Sides of the Law*. New York, NY: Gareth Stevens, 2015.

GLOSSARY

blackmail (BLAK-mayl) to demand money from people in order to keep their secrets
brass knuckles (BRAS NUHK-uhlz) metal rings worn over knuckles to enhance punches
bribe (BRIBE) to pay people money to do things
clans (KLANZ) families
extort (iks-TORT) to get money by force
hits (HITS) killing jobs
illegal (ih-LEE-guhl) against the law
island (EYE-luhnd) land surrounded by water
launder (LAWN-dur) to hide money made from illegal work by funneling it through real businesses
mafia (MAH-fee-uh) organized crime
opponents (uh-POH-nuhnts) groups who compete against each other
outfit (OUT-fit) a group or team
pacts (PAKTS) contracts or agreements
ports (PORTS) areas where ships move in and out
retreat (rih-TREET) to give up in a conflict
rugged (RUHG-id) rocky and uneven
smuggle (SMUHG-uhl) to illegally move things in and out of a country
snipers (SNIPE-urz) sharpshooters who can shoot from a high hiding place from a far distance and with good aim
tattoos (tah-TOOZ) ink drawings on skin
territory (TER-ih-tor-ee) an area that is owned
threaten (THRET-uhn) to warn people by telling them you're going to hurt them
torture (TOR-chur) to cause pain on purpose
tributes (TRIB-yoots) payments made for protection
urban (UR-buhn) city life
victor (VIK-tur) the winner
warriors (WOR-ee-urz) fighters

INDEX